WILBUR AND ORVILLE
AND THE FLYING MACHINE

For Anton

Copyright © 1989 American Teacher Publications

Published by Raintree Publishers

Library of Congress number: 89-3614

Library of Congress Cataloging in Publication Data.

Marquardt, Max.
  Wilbur, Orville, and the flying machine / Max Marquardt; illustrated by Mike Eagle.

  (Real readers)
  Summary: A biography of the aviator brothers, for beginning readers.
  1. Wright, Wilbur, 1867-1912—Juvenile literature.   2. Wright, Orville, 1871-1948—Juvenile literature.   3. Aeronautics—United States—Biography—Juvenile literature.
[1. Wright, Wilbur, 1867-1912.   2. Wright, Orville, 1871-1948.   3. Aeronautics—Biography.]   I. Eagle, Michael, ill.   II. Title.   III. Series.
TL540.W7M36   1989   629.13'092'2—dc19   [B]   [920]   89-3614
ISBN 0-8172-3503-5

  2 3 4 5 6 7 8 9 0   93 92 91 90 89

REAL READERS

Wilbur and Orville
and the Flying Machine

by Max Marquardt
illustrated by Mike Eagle

Raintree Publishers
Milwaukee

One day, in the year 1878, a man named Milton Wright rushed home to his family. He hoped his two little boys Wilbur and Orville would like the toy he had for them.

"Boys! I am home!" Mr. Wright called out.

The two boys, 11 year old Wilbur and 7 year old Orville, ran to meet him at the door. Mr. Wright tossed them the toy. The toy could fly! It was a little flying machine.

In 1878 people did not have TV's or fly in airplanes. There were no such things in 1878. But in many ways, life then was like life now. Children then liked toys, too, just like they do now.

The boys had fun with the new toy for two days. Then, it broke. They tried to make a new flying machine. But their flying machine did not work.

"One day we will fly," said Wilbur.

"Yes," said Orville. "One day, we will."

Wilbur and Orville loved to fly kites. They went with their friends to a high hill. Each boy and girl wanted to have the best kite. Each wanted a kite that would sail high in the sky.

"I know how to make a better kite," said Wilbur one day.

"You do?" said Orville.

"Yes," said Wilbur.

Wilbur showed Orville his plans. The two boys worked hard to make the new kite. It did not look like the other kites.

The boys took their kite to the hill. Their friends looked at the kite.

"That will never fly," they said.

"Yes, it will," said Wilbur and Orville.

Orville pulled at the kite. It sailed up, up into the sky.

"Look at that kite!" said a boy.

"Can you make me a kite like that?" asked a girl.

After that day Wilbur and Orville made many kites. They made kites for their friends.

Wilbur and Orville liked to make new things. They made many new things at home. They found ways to make things better.

When they grew up, they opened a bike shop. There, they made their own bikes. Their bikes were good bikes. They did not cost a lot. People came from all over to get bikes made by Wilbur and Orville Wright.

14

When they were not working in their bike shop, Wilbur and Orville used their time to learn about flying. One way they learned about flying was to look at birds. They saw the birds dip and glide. This gave them ideas for a new flying machine.

"One day we will fly," said Wilbur.

"Yes," said Orville. "One day we will."

The years passed. Wilbur and Orville went on testing their ideas. They made big kites. People came to see Wilbur and Orville fly their kites. Some of the new kites worked well. Some did not.

In 1899, Wilbur and Orville worked on a new kind of flying machine called a glider. After a lot of hard work it was ready. But where would Wilbur and Orville test it?

They needed a place that had a lot of wind. They found a place, far away, in another state.

This place was Kitty Hawk, North Carolina. There, the wind came in off the sea. It would be a good place to test the flying machine.

Wilbur and Orville got on a train for Kitty Hawk, North Carolina. They had a big box with them. In the box were the parts for their glider.

"Soon, we will fly!" said Wilbur.

"Yes," said Orville. "Soon we will."

When they got to Kitty Hawk, Wilbur
and Orville put their flying machine
together. Some people came to see if the
glider would work. It glided over the
sand. But the flight lasted only five
seconds.

Wilbur and Orville went back home. They worked on their flying machine for two more years. They knew that a machine without a motor could not fly for very long. So they put a motor on it. They had made the first airplane!

In December, 1903, they took the new machine back to Kitty Hawk. They called it the Flyer.

"This time we will fly," said Wilbur.

"Yes," said Orville. "This time we will."

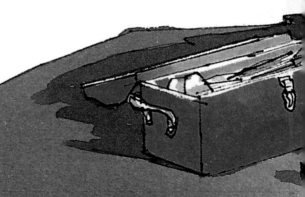

On December 17, the wind was blowing hard. Five men came from town to help Wilbur and Orville. Wilbur started the motor of the Flyer. He went over to Orville and wished him good luck.

Then, Orville got on the Flyer.

Orville was ready. The Flyer began to move. It went faster and faster. Then, it lifted off the ground. Orville was flying!

"We did it!" yelled Wilbur.

The first airplane flight lasted 12 seconds. The Flyer had flown 120 feet!

Wilbur and Orville Wright had worked long and hard. They had dreamed that one day they would fly. And on that day, December 17, 1903, their dream came true.

Wilbur and Orville did not stop working on their dream. They made new machines that could fly longer, faster, and better. Many people saw what Wilbur and Orville did. Then, they too, wanted to fly.

Thanks to Wilbur and Orville Wright and the others who dreamed of flying high, we have fast airplanes. We have spaceships, too. Today people are still working on machines that will fly longer, faster, and better.

Sharing the Joy of Reading

Beginning readers enjoy reading books on their own. Reading a book is a worthwhile activity in and of itself for a young reader. However, a child's reading can be even more rewarding if it is shared. This sharing can enhance your child's appreciation—both of the book and of his or her own abilities.

Now that your child has read **Wilbur and Orville and the Flying Machine**, you can help extend your child's reading experience by encouraging him or her to:

- Retell the story or key concepts presented in this story in his or her own words. The retelling can be oral or written.

- Create a picture of a favorite character, event, or concept from this book.

- Express his or her own ideas and feelings about the subject of this book and other things he or she might want to know about this subject.

Here is a special activity that you and your child can do together to further extend the appreciation of this book: To create an airplane that would fly, the Wright brothers experimented with many kinds of "flying machines," including kites. You and your child can make a simple kite. Take a piece of $8\frac{1}{2}$ x 11 paper. Use crayons or markers to decorate the paper with a large picture (e.g., a butterfly) or abstract design. Cut out the picture. Use transparent tape to attach one end of a ball of string or yarn to the picture. You and your child can fly the kite, or you can display it in your home.